JUMPING THE TRAIN TRACKS WITH ANGELA

PAUL DURCAN

RAVEN ARTS PRESS / DUBLIN
CARCANET NEW PRESS / MANCHESTER

This book is published by

Raven Arts Press   **Carcanet New Press Ltd.**
31 North Frederick Street   210 Corn Exchange Buildings
Dublin 1   Manchester M4 3BQ
Republic of Ireland   England

Copyright © Paul Durcan 1983

Jumping the train tracks with Angela
    1. Title
    821'. 914

ISBN 0 906897-68-8 Soft *(Raven Arts Press)*
ISBN 0 906897-69-6 Hard *(Raven Arts Press)*
ISBN 0 85635-513-5 *(Carcanet)*

Acknowledgements

In Dublin; The Irish Times; The Irish Press (New Irish Writing);
The Cork Examiner; Magill; Quarryman; The Beau; Aquarius;
Poetry Ireland; The Mike Murphy Show (RTÉ Radio 1).

In particular I would like to express my gratitude to the Editor
and staff of *In Dublin* magazine in which various versions of
many of these poems orginally appeared.

Raven Arts Press acknowledges the financial assistance of the
Arts Council *(An Chomhairle Ealaíon)* Dublin, Ireland, in the
production of this book.

Carcanet New Press acknowledges the financial assistance of
the Arts Council of Great Britain.

Typesetting and Layout by Vermilion, Clondalkin, Co. Dublin.
Printing by Confidential Report Printing Ltd., Dublin.

JUMPING THE TRAIN TRACKS WITH ANGELA

CONTENTS

I

II

I

THE MAN WHOSE NAME WAS SHAKESPEARE

I knew a man whose name was Shakespeare.
His first name was William, and he wrote plays
For a living. Pretty daring plays they were too.

Yet he himself lived a quiet life with his tempestuous wife:
They used to go to bed early, they were fond of the bed,
And rise with the sun or more often the mist;
He to his desk, his sonnets, and his plays;
His wild, wild humour like wild, wild whiskey.

They invented games and on summer evenings they played
A species of tennis in the back-garden with the river
On one side, and the jail-house on the other:
When they died — they died together in their sleep —
I served a refrain for them which was one double theme:

Play it deep to the backhand, O Will, will you my dear?
Play it deep to the backhand, although it kills me to run:
Play it deep to the backhand, O Will, will you my dear?
Play it deep to the backhand, although night will come.

THE WOMAN WHO KEEPS HER BREASTS IN THE BACK-GARDEN

Why do you keep your breasts in the back-garden?
Well, — it's a male-dominated society, isn't it?
Yes, I know it is, but could you explain . . .
Certainly, I'll explain, certainly:
Seeing as how it's a male-dominated society
And there is all this ballyhoo about breasts
I decided to keep my pair of breasts in the back-garden
And once or twice a day I take them out for a walk
Usually on a leash but sometimes I unleash them
And they jump up and down and prance a bit
And in that way the males can get their bosom-gaping done with
And I can get on with my other activities.
I used to leave them out at night under the glorious stars
But then little men started coming in over the walls.
I have other things on my mind besides my breasts:
Australia — for example — Australia;
To tell you the truth, I think a great deal about Australia.
Thank you very much for talking to us, Miss Delia Fair.

WATCHING MICHAEL CULLEN'S STRAWBERRY NUDE WITH FRIEND

The stars are black, the night is blue,
Whoever wrote that you are you
Must have been writing with his eyes open;
But as any snowman worth his snow
Will tell you on a North African shore
"A man cannot write with his eyes open:
Like any other Russian,
My dream is to draw my mother's picture from memory;
You can only write with your eyes closed."

The stars are black, the night is blue,
You are all that is not you:
The grave-faced girl in black leather jacket
On a lean Dublin street in ice-cold rain
Is stepping out naked under a North African sun:
Such is her fragile nonchalance,
Such is her shy insouciance,
She is the epitome of the vertical swimmer!
Her prehistoric future! Her stereophonic past!

The stars are black, the night is blue
I must not think that I am you:
I am the eye of the needle through whose strawberry steel
You, who are a strawberry camel, are passing:
When even you're with me, how I miss you!
With what simultaneity you keep your balance
On the Ferris Wheel of Fate! While you laugh at me
Beneath you far below in the fairground!
A cucumber lonely for his strawberry nude!

The stars are black, the night is blue,
There is a palm-tree peering down at you:
A palm-tree with an eye in the top of its head.
I am bright with jealousy, bright with it,
Jealous as the night and the moon is a spacefish
Swimming down into the black mouth of your thigh.
Oh that sky-high palm-tree! What a phallic fellow!
What shoulderblades! What hips! Yet a small conifer
Is courting you, disguised as a parasol!

The stars are black, the night is blue:
What will I do?
Tell the world about strawberry — strawberry you?
But who is your friend with eyes of blue?
It seems to me that you've got a rendezvous
With a snowman in a black djelaba;
I can see the blue eyes in the back of his head
And he is advancing like an empty bed;
No dog is gonna get between him and his strawberry nude!

The stars are black, the night is blue,
I don't understand it but of course you do;
A herd of sleeping zebra, one of whom is me,
Dream of being trampled to death by you:
Out in the desert a strawberry woman
Is giving birth to a tiny strawberry man
While she attends the funeral of a big strawberry man;
On either side of her, concertinas of strawberry men
Queue up to give her a strawberry kiss:
Isn't it strawberry, strawberry, that it's all so strawberry!

There is a life after language! Bury me —
O my strawberry girl — bury me.

THE ROSE OF BLACKPOOL

He was a goalkeeper and I am a postmistress
And the pair of us believed — I say 'believed' — in Valentine's Day:
What chance had we?
(I speak in hindsight, of course:
I would not have spoken like that in front of the Greak Irish Elk
Or, for that matter, in front of a 22" colour T.V.):
What chance had we?
Every chance — and, at the same time, not a chance in the world.

You see, I had my own little Post Office at the very top of the hill
And I kept it completely and absolutely empty except for the counter.
One day he had said: "You are the Rose of Blackpool":
And that night in bed on my own with my head in the pillow
(*Feathers*, I may say — I cannot abide *Foam* —
Nor could *he*)
I whispered to myself: Alright, that's what I'll be,
I'll be — the Rose of Blackpool.

Many's the Valentine's Day that went by
Before I got my hands on a P.O. of my own
But got it I did — and right on top of the hill-O!
And in that bare, spic and span, unfurnished shop
With its solitary counter at the very far end
I stood like a flower in a flowerpot
All the day long — drips & leaves & what-have-ye:
All the year round — *"Number 365, Are you still alive?"*
And when the door of my P.O. opened
(And as the years went by, it opened less and less and less, I can
                                                    tell you that)
The doorbell gave out such a ring — such a peal —
That the customer leapt — stood dead — and I smiled
Until my cheeks were redder than even
        A Portadown Rose in a Sam McCready Dream.

And I had my black hair tied up in a bun
And my teeth — well, this is what my goalkeeper used say —
Were whiter than the snow in Greece when he played a
Game there in nineteen hundred and fifty-three.

The trouble with my goalkeeper was that he was too good of a
                                                      goalkeeper:
He simply would not let the ball in — not even when you got a
                                                      penalty against him.
Now it sounds Funny Peculiar — and it is —
(But then so is Valentine's Day
And all who steer by the star)
But to be a successful goalkeeper in this world
You simply have to let the odd ball in:
Benny would *not* — and so one night the inevitable happened:
We were up in Dublin and the game was being played under lights
And he hit his head off the crossbar making a save
And the two uprights fell across him
And the removals were the next night and the burial was the day after.

Of course, some people say that he's living in Argentina
                                  with a white woman:
(I'm brown, by the way, and my name is Conchita):
But *that's* what *they* say — *what* do *they* know?
I stand alone in my little, old, lofty, and lonely P.O.,
The Rose of Blackpool,
And I do not believe that there was ever another man in the world
Who could court a woman like my goalkeeper courted *me*,
Especially at away matches at nights under lights:
Benny courted Conchita like a fella in a story:
And no matter how many shots he had stopped in the foregoing year
He always — O he always — and he always —
Posted *me* his Valentine.

O Rose of Blackpool, let Mine be always Thine.

GLANMIRE BOY

The gossip is that my mother is a dumpy little woman
But — and I say this although I am not a religious fanatic
Even though I am twelve years of age —
In my eyes she is the Queen of Heaven
As well as the Queen of Glanmire.
Watching her waddle back up from the village
(We live in a ranch-house half-way up the hillside)
I see the Fir Trees step out to woo her:
They step out onto the road and follow her:
And the Glashaboy River climbs up out of its bed
And, hauling itself up over the high yellow bank,
It eels its way after her, tongueing her heels.
Considering that my father —
Who behaves in our house as if he were God —
Is super-cruel to my mother
I cannot understand why she never allows
The Trees and the River into the house.
If I were her
I would allow the Trees and the River to share my bed.
Such company would do her the world of good:
In the mornings she would wake up feeling well with the world
And, in her pillows, snuggle up among water and leaves:
I would bring her up her breakfast on a tray
If she would promise — and I am sure that she would —
To splash me with riverwater and smear me with leaves.
On Saturday afternoons I would go into town early
And stand in the cinema queue on behalf of the four of us:
River and Tree, Mother and I:
And afterwards with my pocket-money
I would treat them all to Tea and Cakes in the Pavillion.
Last year I queued for two hours in the snow
To get the four of us into *War and Peace*.
Oh, if only my father did not exist:
Fathers are what make the world go — not round —
But sideways — sideways in a skid —
A skid that scares the nightlights out of me.

I wake up at 4 a.m. to hear my mother screaming:
At first I think that I am only dreaming:
But then my father in his pinstripe pyjamas,
With white cord knotted in a dicky-bow over his fig-leaf,
Pads into my bedroom and licks me on the forehead
While behind him my mother's tears
Cartwheel in white nightgowns past my door.
He likes to imagine himself as a pedigree blue-and-white bull
With a red rosette between his eyes and a cigar in his gob:
When Mother declines to hang a rosary-beads round his horns
He charges round the bedroom like a Taoiseach.
As I write, Mother is in the kitchen —
That dark basement which to me is the sunniest field:
The premier park in all of Munster:
If I was a painter I would do a nude of her
Which would make the Golden Vale look dull.
She may be dumpy but she is also creamy
With mountain valleys and bottomless lakes
And farms of buttercup, and lanes of whitethorn;
With eclairs in her laughter
And her fingers in her mouth;
Her eyes are essences
And her heart is a bag of flour;
And cups of tea in her ear-lobes;
And polythene bags round her tears:
And Oh the gravy of her chatter —
And Oh the batter of her reticence.
I sit with my backside on the rail of the Aga cooker
While she gives out yards to me for not polishing my shoes:
Ireland seems to me to be a pretty crummy country —
But then every country seems to be pretty crummy:
She is the best news from Cork to Milwaukee
And I am in love with her:
So there now, put your bets on me — Glanmire Boy.

THE PROBLEM OF FORNICATION ON THE BLARNEY CHRONICLE

Yes — well I think that there is far too much fornication going on
At *The Blarney Chronicle.*
Particularly in the Reporters' Room,
And indeed the situation is as bad among the Sub-Editors;
I mean — it is one thing to have fornication in the Reporters' Room
But it seems to me quite another thing — quite another altogether
To have fornication going on to the same or even greater extent
Among the Sub-Editors; and that's not the end of it:
At teabreak this morning (actually I had coffee myself)
One of the Proof-Readers,
An extremely personable and sychophantic chap called Ermanarie Van Dal
(Yes, it *is* a name to play with, isn't it — Celtic I suppose —
Although it is rumoured that he is of Danish extraction
And I should not be surprised if that's the case)
Well, he told me that among the Proof-Readers
There is A Whole Lot of Fornicating Going On;
It sounds like the name of a pop song;
You simply cannot sustain or indeed tolerate fornication on that scale
On a newspaper — certainly not on a serious, low-quality newspaper
The likes of *The Blarney Chronicle*
And, as for the situation in the Typists' Pool, well I mean . . .
The only thing to do is to get hold of the Oxford English Dictionary
As well as of course one's own sexuality —
By the way, have you seen the report sent in by Field three hours ago
On the 28-year old Newry man shot dead in the head in front of his
        kiddies?
A Provisional I.R.A. show, of course;
Horse-Face Durcan wants to run a front-page story on this
But I've had to remind Horse-Face that there's no room on *The Blarney*
On the front page or any other page for this kind of tear-jerker;
It just doesn't jerk anyone's tears anymore;
The dead sod was a Protestant and, besides, unemployed —
As I was saying, we must get hold of the Oxford Dictionary
And look up the word Fornication and, if necessary,
Send for the Gárda Síochána or, at the very least,
Give the Attorney-General's office a buzz — you know the sort of bilge —
"Problem of Fornication in Blarney Castle!
Fornication: yes: F-O-R-N (Forn) I-C-A-T-I-O-N (ication):
No: it's not *pub*lication — it's *forn*ication:
FORNICATION, fuck it."

Look: I know what: the best thing to do
Is for Gordon to write a Sermon on it
(After all there has not been a sermon-writer like Gordon
Since Thomas formulated in the abstract with his wife,
North-west of Anatolia, I think it was)
"Fornication In The Backyard" — sort of thing:
On the other hand, the female journalists in the union chapel
Are all militantly pro-fornication
So that if Gordon leans in an anti-fornication direction
There might well be more pants flying about the place than ever . . .
Frankly, Frank, I don't know what the shite to do:
Strange bag of tricks — fornication — isn't it?
They put that Newry bugger's brains in an envelope for his widow:
At least there is a streak of decency left in the world.

OLD LADY, MIDDLE PARISH

When the small old lady introduced the small old man to me as
"This is my gunman"
I found it awkward to keep my composure:
"Your husband?" — I corrected her for I considered myself
Well-versed in the culverts of colloquial confusion:
"No, sir, my gunman" she smiled a tiny, quiet smile
"We have been married 48 years
And he is the best gunman a woman could have ever had:
If I was to live my life over again,
I would marry the very same gunman".
I peeped at the gentleman
But he only peeped back at me, his eyes wet with merriment,
And his toothless mouth like a knotted-up silk handkerchief,
Orange silk with clusters of black stains on it;
I formed the impression that he was hard-of-hearing
But in any case she chattered on like a lark's party in Mozart:
"He was a faithful gunman all his life
And now we live in a gunman's flat
In North Main Street,
Just enough room for the pair of us,
And just enough to make do
When you add his gunman's pension
To what I scrape myself — I do for Mrs Dunne —
The Mrs Dunne — No 3 Winston Churchill Villas —
Just opposite the back-gates of U.C.C. —
2½ hours Mon, Wed, and Fri —
£2.50 an hour:
I like it but it is a queer rake of a house — the Dunne house —
She keeps Mr Dunne under the floorboards
In an upstairs bedroom:
She says that he sleeps a lot because he thinks he is a mouse:
I have never set eyes on him but now and then
I have heard a faint scratching:
Makes you curious, doesn't it? Curious to know like.
O I am always glad to get home to my own gunman
And after we have had tea and watched telly
— *Coronation Street* or *Fame* or *The News* —

We climb into bed — we have got a huge double bed —
From the Coal Quay — old black brass —
It is so high that I have to give my gunman a leg up
When he does not feel strong enough to take a run at it —
And that is when I am at my happiest — at my most serenest —
Then, and when I am at First Mass on Weekdays & Last Mass on Sundays —
Then, when I am there all alone in the dark night
In the rooftops of my native city —
The hills of Cork city all around me
Like prehistoric babies in their cradles
And the moonshine leaping in the window like the River Lee itself
And my gunman tucked in beside me,
The pair of us back to back;
O my dearly beloved gunman,
Once R.I.C. & I.R.A.; shortly to be R.I.P.,
And out there on the rooftops — the future — like a rooster cock
In the wideawake silence . . . Valentia 1017 millibars rising slowly . . .
God bless him beside me — Oh & the poor world too —
The Lebannon — The Lebannon that I used think was Heaven —
And Belfast too and Derry and Portrush —
My gunman used irritate me but he also used delight me
And now I am — yes I am — I am rising slowly into sleep:
If only the whole world could learn to sleep:
You never know but we might wake up in the morning
And cotton on to ourselves: cotton on to ourselves:
Lord, will we ever cotton on to ourselves? Bog-cotton . . ."

KICKING THE BUCKET IN THE RUE d'ULM

I dropped my name in Paris
But nobody heard it:
I wonder if anybody will have heard of me
When I arrive in Heaven.

I suppose, when one considers the implications,
God ought to have heard of me:
If God has not heard of me
I will have to endure the consequences:

Consequences of treetops in fishponds
And of the closed doors of houses:
Consequences of being left behind at bus-stops
Because we were the only ones to keep in a queue:

Consequences of married couples (male, female, or both)
Who have made their homes on gravel-loaded barges
Advancing towards dried-up canal-locks grown-over with grass
And lock-keepers permanently and rancourously drunk.

I wonder if God is as funny as I am:
If He is it might explain a thing or two:
I wonder if there is a Post Office in Heaven:
"Am In Heaven — Having a Whale of a Time".

A Whale of a Time in Heaven:
Matchboxes cluttered with fishbones;
Music emanating from marbles;
Oceanic teardrops.

What would I miss? Buckets.
How could I sit still without Buckets?
All the pages would fall out of my Comic;
All the hair would fall out of my head.

I crouch in a porch in the Rue d'Ulm
On the coldest day in Hell:
Thank you for the fag — but I'd rather be
Milking my cows on the Champs Elysées.

MADAME DE FURSTEMBERG

O Life — it is so difficult:
Smuggling Chagalls in and out of France
And Botticellis in and out of Italy;
Rolling up Francis Bacon at Heathrow
Or Giorgio de Chirico at Fiumicino
In carpets that are best used only as carpets;
Finding a suitcase to fit the size of a canvas
And enough pairs of old socks to stuff it with;
Or wrapping up a Magritte in yesterday's newspaper
And smacking the custom's man with it playfully on the botty:
God, who is Good if he's God, is Naughty.

But you say, Durcan, that you have no paintings?
Don't worry, I'll tell you about mine;
I have three Picassos — how's that for starters?
Nine Soutines, one Matisse, seven Rothkos, one Kitaj.
But do not be disheartened: Remember also
That even if after a performance of *Caligula*
You get a dose of diarrhoea — the craps, you know —
It's not the end of the world, dear.
There's always yet one more curtain —
One more black lady to say to you:
"Pull up your trousers, sir, and take a grip of yourself."

The trouble with you, Durcan, is that apart from the fact
That you are continually failing to pull up your trousers
You tend to take a grip of somebody else
Rather than to take a grip of yourself;
When you sense that a woman finds you gripping
You take a grip of her and you will not let go
Until you have made of her an immortal foe;
Which is not to say that women are not everything;
They are — which is what most of all I want you to know.
Wherefore is the glory of painting?
My darling boy, women are everything!

THE CRUCIFIXION CIRCUS, GOOD FRIDAY, PARIS 1981

At the sixth station there was a soft explosion
And it was not the frantic swish of Veronica's towel
Scouring the face of the gory Christ
Like a pulped prizefighter slumped in his corner;
Perhaps, I thought, it is the man in the porch
With the pistol in his right hand clasped by his left
Held high above his head pointed into space;
(I had wondered about him on my way in);
It was like the air precipitately being let out of a balloon,
Or the rapid deflation of the bladder of a football:
A tall, saffron-faced lady in long gray skirts
— Barely able to stand on account of her age —
Had urinated by accident into her massive black pants
— "My stage curtains" — as she used call them to her great
                                            grandchildren:
The gold urine trickled slowly, as if patiently, across the
                                            stone flags;
Making a map of Europe on the floor as it trickled —
Trickled until it had become a series of migrations
From Smolensk to Paris:
A urine sample for Dr God to hold up to the light,
Or to be microscopic about
— A clue to the Secret Biology of the Universe —
Or for his wastrel son to muck about in.

Her husband gripped her trembling hand
And with his other hand he adjusted the purple bonnet on her head
To make her look more pretty:
That he should think of that at a time like this,
That he should treat his wife with the exact, same courtesy
As he did when he was a young man courting a princess;
And that she should crawl forth from her bed
To topple like this,
To bear witness in a public church,
To risk all or nearly
In order to stand by the side of the subversive Christ —
These are things that do not make me laugh;
These are things that make me weep stone tears;
In spite of the living scandal of the warring churches,
On the grotesque map of Europe there is a country of the heart.

Fellow catechumens looked down askance at the floor,
Then up at the radiant, tormented faces of the agèd couple:
Why do people of their age and station
Behave like this — they ought to know better —
At the Stations of the Cross and — on of all days — Good Friday?
We had not yet even arrived at Golgotha Hill:
The old pair did not look as if they intended to budge from the pool
In which they stood — out of whose banana-yellow ooze
They flowered and towered like agèd, tropical trees,
All wizened and green, all gray and fruity.

The wife kept her eyes fixed on the Cross of Jesus:
Her husband kept his eyes both on her and on the Cross:
Urine or no urine
They were going to bear witness to today's *via dolorosa*
Right out to the end:
If the fellow under the Cross — a dark-skinned young Jew —
Extraordinarily longhaired, even if it is the fashion —
Could himself keep it up to the end: with blood in both eyes
And on his hands and on his feet, he too was in difficulties —
Difficulties with his bodily functions.
Behind the Jew traipsed the priests and the acolytes
In linen albs and lamb's wool surplices:
Voices whispered from the planets: "And where are your assets?"

When at the eleventh station they crucified Christ
The old man held high his head with glittering eyes
Like a man in the stands at a racecourse
Watching a 20-to-1 winner come home
And his wife holding on to the hem of his raincoat,
Not unused to her husband's gambling coups — a loser in society,
He was a winner in life. If at night she had a blackout
And forgot to say her prayers (ever since the War she'd been having
                                              blackouts)
She could always be sure that he would say them for her;
Such things were unspoken of between them
As now they poked their way
In and out the archipelagos and the peninsulas and the lagoons
                                              of urine,
The rivulets and the puddles,
Until they found the central aisle
From which they gazed up at the stalagmite organ in the far-off loft
Famed for its harpies carved in oak:

During the Stations of the Cross
A family of Germans had been snapping photographs of the organ,
With tripod and flash,
Turning their backs on the ludicrous procession-in-progress.

The old man knew that his wife knew what he knew:
That at the end of the War a German soldier
Had hid in the organ loft
In a nest made for him by the sacristy charwoman.
For 3 weeks he had got away with it until the Parish Priest
— An armchair general in the French Resistance —
Had flushed him out: the pair of them —
The young German soldier and the young French charwoman —
Were shot in the back of the head — collaborators —
No Jesus Christ to make it a trio, or was there? —
And the Parish Priest murmured over his bread and wine
That such things happen, and have to happen, in war:
Just so, just so, — murmured a Communist intellectual,
Bloodred wine seeping out of the stained corners of his mouth,
Le Monde for a napkin on his knee.

By now the Crime of the Urine had been doctrinally detected
And the Sacristan followed the trail up the central aisle,
Up and under the organ loft, round by the holy water font,
Out onto the steps overlooking the Place de la Concorde.
He thought: the guillotine would not be good enough
For people who urinate in churches.
But he consoled himself with the observation that Bonaparte
Had good taste in Egyptian obelisks — painted penises, I should think.

In their crusty old rooms
In the mansards overlooking the Madeleine
The two shaking spouses helped each other to undress:
Having laid their two windowsills
With breadcrumbs for the pigeons,
They climbed into bed into one another's arms,
In an exhaustion beyond even their own contemplation —
Beyond the trees and the water, beyond youth and childhood.
He was the first to fall asleep, his eyelids like forest streams,
And the sun — high in the west over the Eiffel Tower and St Cloud —
Framed his golden white-haired face like a face in a shrine —
A gaunt embryo in a monstance:
As sleep came over her she heard him say in his sleep:

"Delacroix, I must speak with you:
If Jesus Christ has no bed, where does he sleep?
In doorways with Algerian women, isn't that so?"
Which fragrant phrases she glossed
"To keep one another warm — warm as urine".
And in Byzantium she saw the gold urine mosaicize in her sleep-fog
like breath:
A diptych of Madonna and Child — at Birth and at Death.

JARDIN DES PLANTES: SPOUSE TO SPOUSE

"Cruel" — I hear you snarl — "Cruel Sea of Woman"
That I should speak from the bilges and not from the skies;
That I should seek to speak the truth, disconnect the lies;
That I am neither Angel nor Beast but Awkwardly Woman;
Awkwardly Woman; neither Easily nor Simply nor Entirely
Woman but Awkwardly — just Awkwardly — Awkwardly Woman.
You nurse yourself, angrily, angrily; comfortably, comfortably;
With the fantasy of wife as a mountaineering seraphim
Ministering at your bedside, pillowing your goathead,
Concealing your gun in my handbag for you as I did
When I was a good girl. Dear Fred,
I am neither dusky fire writhing in slime, nor white rose
Prayering in sepulchral bed:
I am a menagerie bear, down to my toes;
My toenails, like my buttocks, awash with tears:
On the upside-down bucket of marriage I pirouette —
But for how many more years?
For how many more years, I ask you, for how many more years?

MICHELANGELO ROAD

What? Just a little old Jewish couple in their seventies
In their little old house on Michelangelo Road:
"Would you like a book? Would you like a cup of tea?
We are children, and unto children we shalt return."
The old lady does the talking, and the old man does the smiling:
"He has been cogitating a book on the passage of time:
But that naughty old river outside the window
Is proving to be an almost libidinous distraction.
He says that it has the same effect on him as I did
When I was a girl. Whereas for other men
I was stationary, for Benjamin I was moving:
And now he is having an affair with the River Ladle
Darkly curling in the sunlight outside our window
Instead of writing his tome on the passage of time.
But I am not jealous of the river — I do not flap
My ears at it, for I am happy that Benjamin is happy" —
She laughed like a prehistoric rabbit, unperturbed by the firing squad.

PROFESSOR SORBONNE'S SLIDE-SHOW OF THE NEW PARIS

You see —
this is zee new city.
We
had zee sense
— zee common sense, I suppose —
to erect zee new city
in zee Past
rather than to wait
for to erect it
in zee Future:
and you see —
zee underground carpark eez a good place
to go and to do your rape in:
as for zee children, shucks, they can find their places to play
in zee Loopholes of zee Planning.

They say
that zee women are afraid
of zee new situation
and that may be so
but, on zee udder hand,
zee motorcar is zee mode
of transporte in zee 20th century
and after zee motorcar
there is zee officeblock
and zee apartmentblock:
and so, anyway, you see —
zee underground carpark eez a good place
to go and to do your rape in:
as for zee children, shucks, they can find their places to play
in zee Loopholes of zee Planning.
Do you understand? Good.
Now go to hell, my friend.

OUR LADY OF THE BLACK TREE

In those years I was a handyman in a boy's boarding-school in the centre of the city. Early one winter morning I was working in my toolshed on the edge of the basketball court, all rain-water and sparrows, (or was it a volleyball court?) when I remembered that I had left my power drill in the refectory where I was boarding up a few windows.

I stepped out into the fresh air but as I turned toward the main building (the refectory was on the ground floor) a movement in a tree on the far side of the basketball court caught my eye. Some boys up to some sort of cafuffle, I supposed.

I stopped, stood still, stared. There, half-way up the trunk of a bare, black tree stood a small woman with an infant strapped onto her, hugging her stomach as if to connect its brains with her intestines. Her face was in a state of decomposition and her jellylike flesh was frozen in a petrified howl, and she was wearing a nun's wimple. With her right arm she was pointing emphatically at something in the distance but her left arm was missing.

Later, in the police station on the Golden Road, I was shown the face of an ape photographed in "a state of terror". Yes, it was the same face, I replied to the police. I wondered (to myself but not to the police) if "the state of terror" had been induced partly, if not entirely by the photographer; had the human being with the camera not produced the camera, the ape's face had most likely been in a state of repose.

There was only one other witness — a young woman with short hair and a long oval black face who had been look out the fourth floor window of a book repository in Turkey Street which overlooked the perimiter wall of the school. Apparently she had got into the habit (she worked as a charwoman in the repository) of peeping at me — a detail which touched my male vanity to the quick.

Her testimony was that she had seen "no woman in no tree"; the police told me that she had made her statement with unusual passion, almost anger. She did not advert to the fact, nor did the police draw her attention to it, that the tree had its back to her, and therefore she could not have seen what I saw, real or un-real, chimera or catastrophe. All she saw — as indeed all she ever saw, it seems, when she peeped her daily morning peep from that window — was me.

In any case, as I was leaving the police station, standing on the steps in the winter morning gale, the Police Inspector muttered something about "a dirty drunken bum asleep in the gutter around the corner — curled up like a fucking foetus, if you'll forgive the expression".

Were any, or all three of us, on the ball? Or are we all ego-trippers or, as a happy-go-lucky coroner once put it, pathological solipsists? There is only one point which is plain. Life is an abortion. Our Lady of the Black Tree — have mercy on us.

DEATH IN A GRAVEYARD: PÈRE LACHAISE

The widow was perching by her husband's grave
When a chestnut dropped down onto her skull;
And she, concussed, dropped down onto her spindly knees,
Her forehead glancing off the sharpness of the kerb:
Dead — before you could say Jack Robinson —
To whom she had been married fifty years:
Mrs Robinson poleaxed by a conker:
How she would have laughed — and so would he:
"There I was — decomposing away like mad —
When you collapsed beside me, bombed by a chestnut."

Strollers remarked upon the old lady asleep
In the noonday sun. And so she slept until dusk
And the keepers discovered her, encircled by cats,
A stone circle of cats around their dead priestess,
She who had fed the strays for fifty years
And who had never quarrelled with her prickly husband,
Yet shared with him laughter
Both of the benign bed and of the shaky street.
Only at mealtimes had they been silent; and silence
They had also shared, as if communing in a foreign tongue.
"Poleaxed by a conker, Jack, at the edge of your grave."
"That's the girl, Jill, jump in quick beside me."

THE PERFECT NAZI FAMILY IS ALIVE AND WELL
AND PROSPERING IN MODERN IRELAND

after the painting *Peasant Family, Kalenberg, 1939,* by Adolf Wissel

Billo is the husband and he played county football
For sixteen years and won every medal in the game:
With his crew-cut fair hair and his dimpled blue chin
And his pink, rosée cheeks:
There is a photo of him on every sideboard in the county.
He has five children and he hopes to have five more
And, for convenience, he also has a wife —
Maeve Bunn from Sinchy, 13 miles from Limerick City:
He keeps a Granny in a Geranium Pot on the kitchen windowsill,
An Adoring Granny:
He is a Pioneer and he always wears the Pin;
If he's not wearing a suit he always remembers
To transplant the pin to his bawneen sweater.
He does not dream — except when nobody is looking
Late at night behind the milk parlour
Or in the pig battery with the ultra-violet light-bulb
While the wife is stuck into RTE T.V. —
Dallas or *Quicksilver* or *The Year of the French:*
And he don't like Protestants and he don't like Artists;
Homosexuals —
"Hitler wouldn't be good enough for the likes of them" he giggles;
Lesbians — My God,
A woman making love to a woman
Is as unimaginable and, therefore, impossible
As is a woman having a period
Or giving birth to a babba.
He drives a Volkswagon — The People's Car:
Ein Volk, Ein Reich, Ein Fuhrer.
On Sundays he drives the family mad and/or to the seaside
At Ballybunion in the drizzle;
If any brat in the back of the Volks
So much as gasps
For a window to be opened — just two inches, Daddy —
The heroic driver bestows an enormous clout
On the little head of the gasper;
And he's a County Councillor — whatever that is:

Mind you, he does own a thousand seater pub
For which he was refused planning permission
And from which there is no fire escape —
Which presumably is why he has never been seen on the premises —
The O.K. Corral on the side of the Buggery Mountains.
In bed his wife calls him — yummy, yummy, yummy —
But don't ask me what he works at
Because it doesn't matter what Billo works at:
Billo is a darlin boy and that's all that matters:
All that matters is that Billo is a darlin boy:
All that matters is that Billo is a darlin boy:
All that matters is that Billo is a darlin boy:
HEIL.

INTERVIEW FOR A JOB

— I had a nervous breakdown when I was seventeen.
— You hadn't?
— I had.
— But how could a beautiful girl like you
  Have had such a thing as a nervous breakdown?
— I don't know, sir.
— But you have such luscious hair!
— They said I had some kind of depression.
— With long black curls like yours? Depression?
— Erogenous depression.
— Erogenous depression?
— It's a new kind of depression, sir.
— You're wearing clothes, do you know that?
— Am I?
— You are: I like your lips too.
— My lips?
— Your lips: they're kissable.
— Kissable?
— And your hips: I would say they handle well.
— I beg your pardon, sir?
— Tell me, what kind of man is your father?
— He stays in bed every second week.
— And your mother?
— She stays in bed every second week as well.
— In other words — a happy Irish marriage.
— Why do you say that, sir?
— Well, it's not every husband and wife who go to bed together
  For a whole week, every second week.
— You misunderstand, sir; they take it in turns.
— O.k.: so you want a job?
— Yes, sir.
— Well, you can't have one.
— I beg your pardon, sir?
— You had one hell of a nerve applying for a job.
  You have no right to have a job here or anywhere.
  Get out of my office before I bellow for my Little Willie
  To kick you in the buck teeth and whack you on the bottom.
— Thank you verra much, sir.

— Don't mention it, girrul.
— Well then, sir, d'ye mind if I sit on in your office for 5 minutes: It is terrible cold outside and I have no overcoat.
— Bloody woman, shag off; vamoose; make yourself scarce.
— But, sir, I *am* scarce; my name on the form . . . *Scarcity.*
— Now *Scarcity,* don't act the smart-ass with me: beat it.

TO HER TOY BOY — STEPHEN EVEN

Matrimony is thick with bliss
But do husband and wife ever kiss?
My boyfriend is a married man
Who kisses me whenever he can
Which is not often because I love
The silly-billy: he is a dove,
His wife is a hawk: I am neither —
Which tends to send him up the Khyber.
His eyes are candles lit for Mass
In spite of which he will make a Pass
At me if he sees a chance,
Poor thing. What a dance
He dances when I return the Pass
With interest: "Goddess"
He pants for joy like Archimedes
Discovering Benz in a Mercedes.
Then comes the moment of 'Eureka'
When all his legs become much weaker;
He pants like a doggie. What do wives
Do to their poor husbands' lives
That a mellow fellow like my toy boy
Has become such a randy guy?
If in a shopwindow he sees a bed
He grips my hand and turns puce red
In the ears — a danger sign
Requiring urgent treatment with wine:
My mother purrs "Is that so?"
Concerning all this *vino collapso*.

His face is the face of a man who has suffered:
He told me himself in a hotel in Lifford
(Lifford might be a South Sea Island
Except that it's in the North of Ireland):
I agreed — in the hollows of his cheeks
It has rained not merely for weeks
But for thirty years; his tears
(A tragic shandy of arrears)
Are fossils on my mantlepiece,
But now, dread reader — thy smiles must cease:

This is not the best poem ever written
Even though it's about my kitten —
Stephen Even:
An autumn ode — a kind of leaf-in.
No, there cannot be a more horrible porridge
Than that ice-cold gruel which we call marriage.
Oh learn to Play, and after Play —
Be glad that there is nothing left to say.

THE CHILD ON THE TRAIN, YORKSHIRE, 1980

There was a child in the carriage:
When the train glided out from Leeds
There were only the two of us in it:
Space for both our minds, and space
To bathe our toecaps in the waters of silence.
She was about seven years old, maybe eight,
Long rusty hair and freckled cheeks;
She peered at me, her pink lips sealed;
I strove to read her eyes but I could not.

After York I could bear it no longer:
"My mother was with me at the start of the journey
But after half-an-hour she got out."
"At what station did she get out?"
"She did not get out at a station."

I did not know what to say:
I said: "Well, then, where did she get out
If not at a station?"
                              "She got out
Between stations — it looked
Like a field to me but the train
Was travelling along at such speed
I'm not sure about it."

Not being able to think of anything else to say,
I inquired of her what she would like to be?
"Me? What I would most like to be
Is a horse: do you know any trainers?"

The wide-eyed pun knifed through the air.

Trains — always it has to happen on trains:
Why does it always have to happen on trains?
"She did not get out at a station":
"Do you know any trainers?"

The wide-eyed pun knifed through the air.

THE MAN WHO WANTED TO BE SAPPHO

Some men like to be themselves;
Some like Marlon Brando;
My father did not like himself;
He wanted to be Sappho.

Sappho MacMonagle from Wexford
On top of Nelson's Pillar:
Declaiming the refrain of a new poem
"By God — I'll kill her."

Strong stuff, maybe; but better
Than "I love you":
Was there ever a more perfidious pledge
Than "I love you"?

O the Treachery of Affection!
O the Cruelty of Birth:
Why put a man as man on Earth
If he yearns to be a Lesbian?

Sappho MacMonagle makes love
Like a river in a tree:
Her poems have taken off their clothes
And their hip-flasks of whisky.

No man is an island — but Sappho is:
Dublin in ruins all around her shores.
She lives in one room but she has many doors;
And she puts her arms around you when she goes.

In Mount Street in the rain, O in Mount Street in the rain;
It is the end of the world — it is the end of the world:
But if Sappho is in her long poem, and she answers the door,
She will make love to you on the floor.

Sometimes it is sensational to be a snake:
To interlace with a second snake beneath a desk:
To flow up and over all the furniture in a room:
To disappear — into a coalscuttle in the sun.

GETTING DOWN TO THE REAL PINK

for M.C. and E.J.

It's all slate, it's all brick,
It's all nature, it's all bloody.

Oh I hate you, Oh I hate you;
I hate you; I hate you.

And you could get locked out, and
You could get locked in —
Where would you be then?
Under the lamp'post — compost, if you care to be free —
Under the lamp'post at the Berlin Wall:
Wouldn't that be a nice place to be?
Oh wouldn't that be a nice place to be?
Under the lamp'post at the Berlin Wall?

Never *ad lib:*
It's an ad —
On the Western Side.

Oh I hate you, Oh I hate you;
It's all nature; and; it's all bloody.

FR PEADAR PARTY — THIRD SECRETARY TO THE ARCHBISHOP

What will I do? It is 5.30 a.m. and I cannot sleep
And breakfast is not served after 9.30 a.m.:
The Manageress is ostentatiously toasting herself
                              in her electric blanket
While the Archbishop is snoring franctically
                              in the archepiscopal suite
(The upshot, I suspect, of too many fags and . . .):
Perhaps I should unfurl my purple umbrella
And play a few holes of golf round my room
— Knock a few balls into the wastepaper basket —
Or swat moths with *The Canon Law for Men Only* quarterly?
No — the only cure would be if the Manageress
Would keep out of my bed — but the Golden Age,
Alas, is over — bishops no longer tramp
The goattracks to Compostella —
And the Epoch of the Silicon Chap is at hand.
She — a feminist, would you believe it! —
Would no more keep out of my bed
Than say *Au Revoir* to Adam if she met Adam in the Garden
(Her name is Evelyn, by the way, Evelyn MacNamara:
She had an abortion by Canon Mick Coyle last year
And, the year before that, an abortion by Bishop Tim Green:
MacNamera's Band — they call her in Maynooth.)

Perhaps I should creep into the Archbishop's bedroom
And cuddle his chin — they say that a good cuddle
Cures a bad snore: but he — or somebody —
Might put the wrong construction on my cuddling:
They might think I am bisexual which I am:
Besides, the Archbishop wears a Transistor round his neck in bed —
A Pectoral Transistor:
Oh dearie me, there is nothing for it but to take another overdose:
Oh for the days of the nightly bottle of whiskey under the pillow,
And the dream-music of revenge, and the curer in the morning!
Pure phantasy, purer than the purest of the pure;
Pure, pure, pure, pure.
Oh Purity — Thy Name is Man.

NELL

It was a black May morning — the white telephone rang —
Reluctantly, I picked-up the receiver:
The Third World War had not yet begun —
As far as I knew —
Nonetheless, I was expecting bad news:
My lovey-dovey daddy in Rome perhaps —
"I have just raped your daughter, Shitface:
You can pick-up what's left of her in the Campo de' Fiori."
Lord, Nell, when I heard your voice!
I put down the phone and I ran down the stairs
Jumping three at a time and into the store-room
Where everybody was slaving away at the shelves;
Stacking boxes, sellotaping, labelling,
And longing to God that they were somewhere else
That was not all twilight & dust & reeking of cardboard —
Somewhere in the sun with work to be done —
A cobbled yard with fruit to be humped:
A poker school on the beach with a quorum assembled:
A snooker table in the kitchen and all the girls on cue.
"Hey!" I yelled:
I yelled so loud that they all stopped work
And they stared at me so that I stared at myself:
"Guess who is on the phone asking for you all?"
I whispered —
And when they heard who it was on the phone
You could hear that one name ring out all around the floor,
Up and down the shelves, up and down the aisles,
In and out the trolleys and the buggys and the fork-lift trucks:
It's Nell! It's Nell! It's Nell! It's Nell!
And then and there they all downed tools
— Rubber gloves, shears, tape, paste —
And when Mr Smearfoot the whizz-kid boss-man —
The man with a periwig around his periwinkles
And a toupée glued to his chest —
Sneered through his adenoids "Where are you going?"
They chuckled into his stapled snout and they wailed:
"Down to meet Nell — for Nell has come home
And never again will we slave for you:
Nell has asked us all to come down to meet her:
And to work for her in the valley."
Lord, Nell, when I heard your voice!

RORY CARTY AND SON: HIGHCLASS BUTCHERS

Mammy, why does it say over our front door —
Rory Carty And Son: Highclass Butchers?
Well, son, the key phrase on our shop front is 'And Son':
You are a little boy — that's to say, a nicens little boykins
With a nicens little knocker on your own little front door.
In other words, you are not a little girlyboots.
Your Daddy, whom you adore, abhors little girls
And so, by being a butcher, he combines business with pleasure:
He buys the best little girls that money can buy
— From Santa Sabina and Mount Anvil and the Holy Faith —
And having slaughtered them in his very own abbatoir
(Which used be an aviry when we first got married —
He was bonkers about budgies and canaries and home movies —
Mammy reading *Life* magazine on our honeymoon —
Mammy reading *Time* magazine in our back garden —
Mammy reading *Woman's Own* in the Phoenix Park —
Mammy with an overcoat over her swimsuit —)
— Having slaughtered them in his very own abbatoir
He hangs the little girls in the freezer for 14 days
(Just like it's done in *The Robespierre Hotel* in Galway)
Before carving them up into choice cuts for the clients
— Psychiatrists, business consultants, art critics,
Economists, poets, developers, architects.
I pray to Our Lady of Fatima that when you're a big boykins
You will become as highclass a butcher as your bloody daddy:
Butchery is such a secure profession for a nasty wee laddie.

THE BALKAN GRILL

Waiting for him to come home.

What was it that came between us?
No one knows what it's like to go on alone
Or, as a girl, to grow up with no father
Lonely as light — and down at the corner
It is getting dark outside *The Balkan Grill:*
He phoned that he has to attend a union meeting,
That he will not be coming home.

Nobody to sing me a lullaby,
My colouring book and me;
Nobody to sing me a lullaby,
My colouring book and me.

The Balkans —
What on earth are The Balkans?
Where are they — The Balkans?
He fancies himself as a clever professor:
"The Balkans? The Balkans are the Genitalia of Europe."
From his side of the bed he growls ex cathedra:
"In spite of the Convenience of Matrimony
We must not balk at Balkanization."

Tomorrow I will take a bus to the zoo
And apply for admission:
Take this cup of tea from my paw
And let me become the monkey that I was;
The wise, old monkey whom I long to be;
And a cage of my own with adequate trees
On which to do my hang-ups:
You may watch me at my hang-ups through the windowpane
And you may say what you like about my hang-ups
Provided that I do not have to answer you,
That I am not obliged to bawl back at you.

An orang-outang under analysis.

The years break up like faces in tears;
               and in the rain
The deserted mother has the pathetic pluck
To light up a votive candle in her battered head:

Lay down a lullaby
For Irinaland and me;
Lay down a lullaby
For Irinaland and me.

I remember a group of people in a café
— 'The Wireless Group' — they were called:
In remembering them, I remember an era —
An era the remembrance of which is of something very personal.

Oh Cyril, I feel ill:
It is dark, it was always dark, in *The Balkan Grill.*

THE NIGHT THEY PUT JOHN LENNON DOWN

The night they put John Lennon down
    Off came my record dealer's lid:
"A pity the bugger did not die
    Three weeks before he did":
Oh John, in the era of record crap,
    It was always good to hear you;
To hear behind your steel voice,
    Your smile a-breaking through.

My record dealer was sad because
    He was almost out of stock,
And all the money that could be made
    With Christmas on the clock!
In death, in life, you beat them all,
    The dealers you would not woo:
And we glimpse behind your granny specs,
    Your smile a-breaking through.

The night they put John Lennon down,
    The night flew out John Lennon's head:
In light John Lennon to the night said:
    "Oh what is your name, Poor Night?"
"M'name's Chapman" twanged the night,
    "An' Chapman's a codename, Mark *you*":
"Imagine!" — wept John Lennon,
    His smile a-breaking through.

The night they put John Lennon down,
    Pat stepped out with Bríd;
And on General Hackett Esplanade
    To John Lennon they paid heed:
The waters bid the ships be still:
    "I will freeze fridges, I will love *you*,
Like walls like bridges" — Bríd sang to Pat,
    Her smile a-breaking through.

The night they put John Lennon down,
 I heard an old man cry:
"O where is the boy? O where is the boy?"
 And he gave the sky a black eye:
An old woman came out of a house
 And, John, she was the image of *you:*
"Old man, the boy is not yet born" —
 Her smile a-breaking through.

The night they put John Lennon down,
 A girl clung to a street corner
Crooning an old oriental number:
 "Oh, My Accidental One":
The affrighted river whispered to her
 "You threw me five pounds, did you?"
She replied — "Here's ten pounds change" —
 Her smile a-breaking through.

The night they put John Lennon down
 I heard a third woman call:
That the only truth a leaf knows
 Is that it's going to fall:
Oh John, it was a moving thing
 That a lonely heart like you
Should perceive behind a woman's tears —
 Her smile a-breaking through.

Change, Changer, Change: Fall, Faller, Fall.

PAPUA, NEW GUINEA

On discovering that his girlfriend had done a bunk to Papua, New Guinea
Micky MacCarthy phoned C.I.E.,
And requested permission to prostrate himself on the Tralee to Dublin line
So that he could behead himself by means of the afternoon train.
"Certainly – Ná Caith Tobac" replied C.I.E.:
"Certainly – Prostrate Yourself – Do Not Smoke."

However, as happens with C.I.E.,
The afternoon train was delayed for 8 or 9 hours
(Only the previous week it had been delayed for 2 or 3 days)
And as Night in the Western Hemisphere
Commenced to spread oe'r earth with starry and sable mantle
Micky MacCarthy felt rather cold
And in the end after making trebly sure that nobody was looking
And that his pants were properly buttoned-up
He repaired to Cissy Buckley's pub
At Lemass Cross
Where right now he is filtering his cranium with whiskey
And beginning to see the world including Papua, New Guinea
In a slightly different light.

THE HARPIST

May Moriarty came of well-to-do stock:
Private tutor, boarding-school, college of music;
When news percolated home
That now she was a harpist with the London Philharmonic
Nobody was surprised, the hat fitted:
She under a great harp in the Royal Albert Hall
For ever, and ever, and ever;
A gilded eternity of dress circles;
Ad saecula saeculorum amen.

But it was not to be:
At the bright age of thirty
May Moriarity came home:
And planting her harp
On the sidewalk of the busiest street
She stayed there thirty-five years
For the remainder of her life.
People could not make her out
Although they poked and pried:
It wasn't the drink and it wasn't the nerves
Although it should have been the one
Or the other, or both.
Shame on her, whinnied the gentility,
But they could not by-pass her
Without furtively slipping a coin
Into the gaping satin purse which hung
From the bowsprit of her harp;
Few dared look her in the eyes
She looked so proud, so windswept
In her music which she played in all weathers,
Winter and Summer, Autumn and Spring;
And she took root for ever in the minds
Of generations of children:
A great, white, stranded, female whale
Plucking harp-strings in a gale.

VINCENT CRANE — THE ENNISKERRY BRAT

He was a man who knew he was a woman
Deprived of even the rights of being a woman;
He would give birth to no children on this earth.

Of all human beings I have known
Vincent Crane was the most distraught;
He knew it, yet he contrived to smile.

Daylight — he would walk out the cliffs,
Boys with pistols creeping behind him,
Girls with knives sauntering towards him:
Yet he would not bother to look behind or before him
But he would peer to either side and rejoice
In the cattle in the sea, in the yachts in the field:
Cruel — that when a woman deserts a man —
He has not even the solace of carrying her child.

MOTHER'S BLUES

And I would if I could but I cannot, son,
Follow you down to the river.

I remember the night he was born
Thirty-nine years ago
In a room in a basement in Hatch Street:
When the midwife flourished him
High up in the candlelight,
Brandishing him in a makeshift forceps
(The War was on — which, come to think of it,
Was not unusual — is there ever a time
When the War is not on?)
Anyway,
When the midwife produced him
He got all red in the face,
Puce,
And the gynaecologist barked: "Stick him in ice":
Oh, he was a quick-thinking gyny, he was:
You think I am joking — but I am not joking:
They put the wee bairn in an ice-pack for 14 days
And if I had been at his christening
(I was not permitted to attend
Because I was a woman
With a head on me — "You can only come
If you leave your head at home
And bring 2 pairs of bosoms with you" —
Whispered Bishop Ballsbridge to me)
— If I had been at the christening of my son,
I would have had him christened "Snowfire":
Wouldn't that have been a pretty name?
Snowfire — Snowfire Connolly:
If you listen to it slowly — Snowfire —
It makes Sapphire sound like Sludge.

MAN FOUND DROWNED IN RIVER SUIR

O Son of Woman, where have you gone,
Nocturnal in the sun?

Under the water, under my hand:
So near, so dear, so far away:
And I would if I could but I cannot, son,
Follow you down to the river.

And I would if I could but I cannot, son,
Follow you down to the river.

THE SUN ALSO DOES NOT RISE

Fiesta in a Dublin city street on a hot June night,
Pavements spreadeagled with wild mountain heather –
All of James Plunkett's trumpets and eaglefeather.

He ran into her, and she into him:
They did not stop running until they got to her flat:
And when they awoke in the same bed in the morning
He concluded that they would live henceforth together.
"Oh no, we will not" she smiled, and a seagull
Creaked outside the window: "Why not?" he queried:
"No why" she smiled "we just never will."

At noon he zig-zagged with her back into the city:
At the traffic lights she spun to cabaret *Goodbye:*
He implored her not to cabaret *Goodbye:*
But she cabaret'd *Goodbye,* nevertheless, *Goodbye.*

He agonized then, and for 12 years after,
Did it all have to do with her being a doctor?
He crawled across the rooftops of the years,
Down along the desolate, magnetic valleys,
Beholding her ghastly face in dormer windows:
But either she could not hear him, or she did not want to,
When he yelled, and he mimed, and he gesticulated.

Brown-eyed Fiona, face over golden face,
Did it all have to do with her being a doctor?
That was the one question he had not dared ask her:
Did it all have to do with her being a doctor?

Well, I am not ashamed of the tears in my eyes:
Ernesto, *ciúnas:* the sun also does not rise.

AND I SAW IN THE WINDOW NIETZSCHE WITH HIS CUP OF TEA

And I saw in the window Nietzsche with his cup of tea:
All alone — alone in the night world:
The smile on his lips was the smile of a man
Conjoined with a woman in the act of coition:
Imagine the smile on the lips of the woman
Receiving all that she asked for, and more;
Nietzsche blinked — flocks of smiles flew out of his eyes;
He scratched one lobe, he scratched the other lobe,
Unlatching flocks of smiles out of both of his ears;
And, tweaking his nose, yet more flocks flew out of each nostril,
Splitting the septum;
He anchored his rust-eaten hands on a blue globe of the world
Before he clasped them in a church-steeple on which to pray his chin:
Such ecstasy on the face of a professor was amazing news to me:
I departed — having seen in the window Nietzsche with his cup of tea.

BOGSIDE GIRL BECOMES TAOISEACH

All the Girls of the Tree cascading over the Street of the Stream
In skin-tight cloud-silver jeans
— Like autumn leaves —
Herding their hips behind them,
Five metres behind them;
Their breasts breaching the air
Five metres in front of them;
Their heads held high
At zero;
Their hands behind their necks,
Their laconic necks.

A danger to traffic?
An ideal danger to traffic
— Like a leaf-storm. —
Personally, I would like to see all the young women of the world
Bring the old world to a standstill
And cause such a jam that every man
Would have to abandon not only his car
But himself: let the girls take over —
And the new world begin.

SCREWBALLS

None of them know that the tiny, old tramp
Who hobbles in everyday to the supermarket
Is Professor of Dogmatic Theology at the Institute:
He limps so heavily that they say he has a twisted waist,
A twinset of liquidized hips,
And he is such a dwarf that some say he is a midget;
And his soup-stained blue overcoat reaches down to his toes
So much so that you can scarcely see him,
Scarcely see the tomato red nose under the snowy hair;
And his eyes hang out of his skull on long bits of blue string;
And what's left of his hands are concealed under pendulous cuffs.

They allow him to hobble straight up to the till,
In spite of the queue:
Day in, day out, he makes the same purchase —
A carton of 12 jam rolls:
And as out of the supermarket he crawls away,
An edible snail hypersensitive to his fate,
A slug tuned-in to his own slime,
The checkout prima donna shrills:
"There goes our own local tramp — Screwballs;
He hasn't got a brain in his nut, poor thing."

Back in his attic cell in a grimy 18th century block
The Professor of Dogmatic Theology takes down from
                                        the dust-lapped shelf
The *Confessions of Saint Augustine*
And, employing it as a portable table with which to catch the crumbs,
He crouches on the edge of his narrow bed, nibbling the rolls:
"Tonight I will say the *Hail Mary:*
That is what I will do: no books."

Meanwhile, 3 hours to go until dusk:
So hang on to your seats — just as Screwballs
Is hanging on to the edge of his bunk
Waiting for dusk to come and blow him away:
Listen to Screwballs, red jamroll on his black, blistered lips:
Hail Mary, full of grace, the Lord is with thee . . .

Screwballs soon will be with *Thee*
In a babby's coffin on a black trestle:
Blessed art thou among women, and blessed is the fruit of thy womb.

THE ELEPHANT HOUSE IN BERLIN ZOO

I am an old woman too weak to sleep.

I sit in the Elephant House of Berlin Zoo,
Alone with a herd of Uganda elephant:
I sit here most of the day with them;
And, if I could, I would sleep with them
Or, at least, be their nightnurse:
Reverberations of a lifetime;
A stampede of gentleness.

I know what it is like to be caged:
To be a teen-ager in a bicycle shed:
To be a big girl stranded in a bedroom:
The Afghan loneliness of windows;
The Kabul finality of suicide.

How I crave to stroke their pinned-back ears:
To caress their leatheriness:
To massage their pink parts:
To attend to their trunks.

Closing-time
And I put away my Bible:
A unicornlike rhinoceros is unloading gallons of urine,
Gold urine,
Into a trough the size of a double-bed:
With all the finesse of a heavy rainshower.

I can see also through the glass wall behind me
A couple older than myself
Cuddling on a bench:
Earlier today at the terminus
I saw the 60-year old driver of the No 84 bus
Embracing in the back seat with a lady on his knee.

If I could live my life again
I, who all my days have been a refugee,
Would rather have been a Uganda Elephant
Than a Berlin Woman.

That's the Girl, Big Ears,
Smile for the camera-squads:
Curtsy for the telescopic lens:
Sink down to your knees into the long grey grass.

I am a blank
On which only Death can put a face:
Am I a — was I ever a — member of the race?
Oh my darling Mozart:
I close my eyes and I behold you
Washing your piano fingers in gold urine.

JUMPING THE TRAIN TRACKS WITH ANGELA

The hotel is walking down the street,
Hoping we look the other way;
We will have nowhere to sleep tonight;
Nothing will ever be O.K.

The world was only the world when she was there:
Yet in the railway station bar
There was nobody more disconsolate there than she;
I observed her big-eared smile in silhouette;
Her voice poised in the short grass of her hair:
In jail I know bright hours when I recall
Jumping the train tracks with Angela.

First Love comes always Last.

In the railway station bar
She hummed an air I do not know;
The other tables and the people at them
Come back into the frame because she was there;
When she went out, so too did they;
In jail I know bright hours when I recall
Jumping the train tracks with Angela.

First Love comes always Last.

Despite the weather and the danger
She liked to stop and look around her:
We stopped and looked at a loco engine
Shunting backwards into a coach;
Until the coupling was complete,
She kept her arms around my waist;
In jail I know bright hours when I recall
Jumping the train tracks with Angela.

First Love comes always Last.

Sunlight scarpered along the platform,
Pursured by hailstones with grey hats;
When Angela asked me for protection
I conceded I am myself a racket;

She laughed away my coy chicanery;
She proclaimed to a goods train that I too was good!
In jail I know bright hours when I recall
Jumping the train tracks with Angela.

First Love comes always Last.

She was so sad she could not keep her balance;
She did not notice that I held her hand;
She could not remember her own name —
She who came first in Ireland in Maths Physics,
She who had never savaged a soul;
Oh in jail I know bright hours when I recall
Jumping the train tracks with Angela.

First Love comes always Last.

Alone I went back into the bar; an old nurse there
Disclosed to me that in Heaven they speak Russian;
But — she added — It's the same in Hell:
I sat at the counter staring at bottles of vodka,
Hearing only Angela's brusque *Goodbye:*
Oh yet in jail I know bright hours when I recall
Jumping the train tracks with Angela.

First Love comes always Last.

THE CHILDREN OF HIROSHIMA, DUBLIN 7

In Prussia Street she bought a house;
A three-storey house with half a roof;
One night we chanced to meet in O'Connell Street;
I inquired if she required help to put back the roof.

O we were acquaintances — we were not lovers;
We stood on the roof and ate our lunch;
After nine months she remarked to me:
"Well now that we have got a roof to stand on —

You might like to have a roof over your head:
Would you care to share the same roof as me?
We are total strangers, know each other well,
To me you are just like dirty old bronze."

"Is that a smile on your face?" I said to her:
"Yes, I think it is" — she did but frown:
The sky of her face was a fire on the sea:
She ran out the back — "I'm gone to get fags."

As I clambered upstairs I had not much time:
In her bedroom I looked at myself in the window:
I saw the mental hospital behind her garden wall:
A kind of football match was going on.

O Jesus — this house is where I yearn to live:
This is the human being with whom I yearn to live:
O Jesus Gypsy — tell me her fate:
Before she comes back through the back-garden gate.

Am I a criminal, awake in the nightmare,
To break into the life of a stranger in Prussia Street?
Jesus — He looked like a Cuban revolutionary — He smiled:
"What's at stake is her heart and not your head."

The football match was upside down:
So upside down that it looked perfectly alright:
Then she came in the door smoking a cigarette:
I stammered: "My name is Joe Cross and I love you."

She waltzed rapidly past me to the mantlepiece:
Tapped the ash of her cigarette into the wrought-iron grate:
Spun around with a smile on the bridge of her nose:
"My name is Nuala Quinn — who are you, strange boy?"

And she threw her arms around me like a slow
Black breeze around a block of flats;
And as we watched the football match in the mental hospital
We sat together on the edge of her bed:

We neither of us were afraid despite the approaching storm:
We exchanged X-ray photographs of each other's scarred bodies:
We had no choice but to go back scarred into Eden:
First, to learn how to sit together on the edge of her bed.

In Prussia Street there is a house
With a goldfish bowl on the window-table:
And on the floor, close up to the ceiling,
Two lovers float, dead as dead can be:

Of what they did die — we do not agree:
'Of romantic love' — the politicians lie:
'Of nuclear fall-out' — the doctors testify:
'They always kept their windows open" — the neighbours whisper.

In the Holy Faith Convent I stab a girl in the back;
In the Christian Brothers School I slap a boy in the face;
In Eden a priest puts a gun to the head of a nun;
In Hiroshima the bent trees listen to familiar footsteps.

In Prussia Street there is no blue plaque
On the blue house, love, where we did live:
We were against war: We were for blue:
Hiroshima is not, and never was, new!
                    Hiroshima!

THE LAST BUS TO BALLYFERMOT

Last night in The Kentucky Grill in O'Connell Street
I asked her to marry me and she turned me down!
But she announced that she liked me and since I was hung up on her
I asked 'Will you live with me?' but again she renounced me!
You can imagine how I felt when I took the lid off the teapot
And, to the accompaniment of the harpsichord of her laughter,
I fork-lifted up from the riverbed two sodden tea-bags:
She sang *Planxty Ó Riada* and *Buddy Holly's Lament:*
But what finally put the kybosh on last night was that I missed
The last bus home to Ballyfermot.

A bus-stop on the quays of the Liffey at midnight!
What an ideal location for the funeral of a friendship;
For the burial of a crane. Knowing that she was pally
With some brilliant young film-makers about town
I speculated in my paranoia if she had ear-marked the location!
That my offer of marriage was a drink she would not swally
Had not stopped her from saying – 'I will walk you to the bus':
We walked along Bachelor's Walk (I am not making this up)
Until on Ormond Quay she declared: I am afraid you have missed
The last bus home to Ballyfermot.

What makes you so fructifyingly sure? – I yelled at her:
My dander was up and there is no more embarrasing spectacle
Than that of a jilted gander with his dander beak-high:
Foaming at the ankles, foam ballooned and oozed out my shoes:
Purple in the earlobes, the Chubb Alarm in my neck had gone off
And, since it was connected up with every Gárda Station in Dublin,
There was not a patrol car in sight, not a guard on the beat:
O desolate bus-stop! Not a sinner except for a saint of the night
Scavenging the trash-cans for carrier-bags: Have you missed – he cried
The last bus home to Ballyfermot?

'You will have to stay with me' – I hoped she would say:
Instead she said – 'I will walk you up along the quays':
Which of course was sweet of her but it made meatballs of me:
With a Life-Sentence on my head I was climbing the landings:
Inns Quay; Arran Quay; Ellis Quay, Wolfe Tone Quay:
At Parkgate Street we came to the parting of the ways

And, when I asked her to sleep the night with me in the Phoenix Park
So that waking in the morning we would be ashes together, she replied:
Life is a bowl of cherries, love, that is why you are always missing
The last bus home to Ballyfermot.

And she flew on one wing up Arbour Hill where there's lashings
of ashes and cherries;
And she flew on one wing up Arbour Hill where there's lashings
of ashes and cherries.

48 HOURS IN BED WITH JOANNA

Driving home through the rain from our seaside hotel
We did not speak to each other:
After 48 hours in bed together
We had grown to like one another.

In one another's arms, we can do no wrong

Through the graves of Glendalough we drove
Weeping for what can, and cannot be:
For the tragedy of the sun, for the victory of the sea;
For the spectacular loneliness of you and me.

In one another's arms, we can do no wrong

She works night-shifts in the sugar factory;
I work days in a motor-cycle shop
Servicing Yamahas, yearning to flop
Down once again beside her in the top —

In one another's arms, we can do no wrong

In the top floor of the hotel by the sea:
She taught me to swim with her in the deep;
And she gave to me the gift of sleep;
Behind her closed eyes the fish do reap —

In one another's arms, we can do no wrong

— Reap freedom from the baited hooks of the tribe;
From lobsters in black blazers with red crests;
Reap freedom to swim among her breasts;
She swimming the breast-stroke in my nests.

In one another's arms, we can do no wrong

48 hours in bed with Joanna:
She was a blackberry.
She thought I was Finn — not McCool but Huckleberry:
But she was a blackberry.

In one another's arms, we can do no wrong

In one another's tongues, in one another's lips;
In one another's caves, in one another's creation;
In the squalid bar of Ireland's most squalid railway station
The bar-girl called for a celebration.

In one another's arms, we can do no wrong

The bar-girl announced us as newly-weds
And she inspected us as if we were flowers:
After being in bed with you for 48 hours
I know now who are the Big Powers:

In one another's arms, we can do no wrong

The Big Powers are not the Nation States:
The Big Powers are you and me
And the 99% who are not free:
In you for 48 hours, I was me.

In one another's arms, we can do no wrong

Inland again, and the Dual Carriageway of Pain:
Such Rain! She smiles out of a downpour of Goodbye;
She is a woman who did not lie;
Her black-and-white face above me when I die:

In one another's arms, we can do no wrong.

MAKING LOVE IN MERRION SQUARE

It is half-past six on a hot June night
In Merrion Square, Dublin 2:
With *The Irish Times* beneath their heads
On cut, virgin grass two lovers roll
Like rolled-up carpets on a showroom floor;
Past them along an uphill, transverse path
A tall young woman pushes her boyfriend in a wheelchair,
The Irish Times in his lap unopened;
On a bench a lady in a yellow dress crosses her knees
And, unfolding *The Irish Times,* begins the Personal Column;
The Personal Column is her glass of poetry
While she waits for time to pass before going home to her flat;
On the adjacent bench a man with no home to go home to
Deploys *The Irish Times* for a quite different purpose:
Past them tip-toes a barrister in his late thirties
Who holds his rolled-up *Irish Times* like a policeman's baton
Or a sjambok which from time to time
He flails on his knee or in the empty air,
Making everybody jump a little, twitch one way or the other:
Irish Times or no *Irish Times*
All eyes, whether in the back of the head
Or at the side or at the front,
Are on the brace of lovers rolled up like carpets,
The female hand like a label adhering to the spine of the male;
And the boy in the wheelchair says to the girl behind him,
Pushing him uphill into the sun:
— I never knew Merrion Square was like this:
    It is so green, such trees, such flowers:
    And the tall, Georgian houses all around the park
    Like crowds in the stands at a football match.
    Can you imagine W.B. Yeats peering down at us now?
    No curtains for him, I bet you, stroking his chin,
    No Venetian Blinds;
    Nor would he scruple to train his binoculars on us,
    His Japanese binoculars:
    And Sheridan Le Fanu and Oscar Wilde: Oh Cuff!
— What is it, Coper?
— Just think of it, and to think also
    That where you are wheeling me now
    A bloody grey cathedral might now be looming

If the Archbishop of Dublin had had his way:
He wanted to erect a cathedral in Merrion Square.
— And would not that have been a grand thing, Coper!
You would make an excellent side-chapel, Coper!
How they laughed in the salt spray of one another's eyes!
She felt she came alive when she was with him:
He with her:
In storms of melancholia or anti-cyclones of affection:
Such as when on this June evening in Merrion Square.
— Come on Cuff, push me — Coper gasped into the sun:
— Push me hard and I will be able to freewheel.
She stood back and watched him roll downhill to the gate,
Terrified that anything might ever separate them.
(sing) *From the waist down; O Lord; from the waist down;*
I'm not lonely anymore Lord from the waist down.

THE LONG-HAIRED BOWSIE

I cared about what Violet thought
And, in any case, I was over the moon about Violet;
But it was not until she called me a long-haired bowsie
That I realised that I was a long-haired bowsie.

All my life I had been a long-haired bowsie!
To think of it: a long-haired bowsie!
For 18 years I had been a long-haired bowsie
And I did not rate my chances of longevity

To undo 18 years of being a long-haired bowsie.
A long-haired bowsie, brimful of nothing;
Even before Violet had said what she had said
I had been feeling that I was dying noisily of nothing.

I stop at a shop-window and affecting an intellectually
Passionate interest in a window-display of knick-knacks
I size-up my skull in the double-glazing:
Ah yes, unmistakeably — the skull of a bowsie:

And not just any old bowsie but, as Violet had said,
(And she wrote it down too — in a letter from Nairobi —
An old man with a flywhisk on the postage stamp —
Her handwriting which makes me seize up with suspense —

Her slanted, curved handwriting in black bic biro):
But a long-haired bowsie — the kind of bowsie
You would see at a poetry reading or a jet-set barbecue:
In an old anorak held together with cord and nappy pins.

Oh how I would like to pin the blame on my father:
To say that because he reared me as a pedigree dog
(He used enter me in shows in Dublin and London
And when he took me out for walks in Herbert Park

He used rig me out in casual gear:
New blue anorak, quality cord and nappy-pins:
He unleashed me near the pond and I scattered to the winds
Small boys who howled while their toy-yachts bobbed

On the rim of the universe, and I reared up
Over the kerb of the pond and I could see my dogbarks —
Pre-electronic cacophony whipped-up by my father —
Mirrored in the waterlily surface of the pond)

To say that because my father reared me as a pedigree dog
I am what I am — it is not so:
"All you want a woman for is to cut your hair:
That is why you are a long-haired bowsie" —

Thus writes my dear, sweet Violet from Nairobi;
She will be back home soon but not to me;
She will not let me kiss her, I will have to kiss her alone:
O Violet, Angel! What can a short-haired bowsie like me . . .

AN EPIC OF UNREQUITED HATE

It is a long time since I have seen Níamh Donnycarney in such great form:
The reason is that she is seething with contempt for the boy next door
— Jerry Glenageary — who sends her a lovepoem by post every day.
When she scowls at him — and, oh boy, she has a prize scowl —
A scowl like the saddle of a 1937 bicycle —
A scowl with a crossbar —
All he does is to look down at the ground
As if the ground was a soulmate of his.
Maybe the ground *is* a soulmate of his —
He spends buckets of time looking down at it in the graveyard,
Pacing up and down with a chaos of smiles on his face,
As if somebody was playing a syntheizer inside his head.
But why does Níamh Donneycarney — such a nice and awkward girl —
Despise Jerry Glenageary — such a nice and awkward boy?
Well, I cannot think why —
Except perhaps that he has three heads.
He had seven heads when he was born
But the obstetrician managed to cut off four — leaving Jerry with three.
Apparently Níamh would prefer a boy with two heads.
As for Jerry he is crazy about Níamh
Because of the canals of her eyes:
Along derelict towpaths Jerry goes out walking the canals of her eyes:
Everything in the Empire of Love — especially love — dies.

WORLD CUP '82 WITH SHEILA

Just so long as this hotel don't go on fire . . .
I mumbled serenely as you lay on top of me
In our seventeenth-storey bedroom in Seville:
5.30 a.m. — a new morning already beginning.

I was on fire and you were on fire
So out of control that we were in control:
Not needing the greed to make love:
Without being aware of it, we were making love.

Silently, we made love with sleeping muscles
We had not used since days of childhood:
In the backs of our arms, in the backs of our legs:
We were in a school gymnasium, on the high bars together.

You permitted me to kiss you under each ear
And in the small of your back and on each wrist;
And with your teeth you kissed me on each shoulder
And, smothering my face in the pillow,

Again you lay on me with such spiritual prowess —
Like a feather on a windowsill in a gale:
I whispered: "What makes Brazil unlike every other team?"
You whispered: "They are used to the heat, I suppose."

O Sheila, let us not go back to Dublin:
Blue-and-yellow girl, let us live in sin:
Far from home, and we will tell no one:
You are my Brazil, and I want you to win.

I want you to beat me 12 goals to nil:
I want you to kick the ball through my net:
I want you to bend me and curl me and chip me:
I want to wear your shirt, and you to wear mine.

Making love in the night in Seville is sweet
But waking up in the morning together is sweeter:
To make sleep with you for the rest of my days:
That is my life's goal now — the cup and the world to me.

You swerve inside me underneath the sheets:
Your tears are raining into the field of my chest:
"Fool" you whisper, "but you are a fool I believe in:
I will marry you, if you will marry me now.

In this space-age bedroom I ask this of you only:
That you mean what you say when you say —
To make sleep with you for the rest of my days:
Brazil loves you, and you love Brazil,

But Brazil is a big girl and her pockets are empty
And Brazil has had her back to the wall so many days and nights
She has wanted to die: to live is her dream —
And to sleep in your sleep until the last execution."

I put my arm around you but you are not there:
You have left the field of play — is the game over?
In a mirror in the dressing-room you light up a cigarette:
Chief Smoking Woman — and Smile of our Tribe:

"The game is never over — that is why it is a game:
Fly by Silk Worm, Crawl the Ocean,
And we will play sex football in the Mato Grosso.
Let us arm in arm get scared to death in Rio."

But will you head me off the line, love, will you head
                                    me off the line?
O yes — you are mine, love, cream of the swine.

BROTHER, CAN YOU SPARE A VALIUM?

Brother, can you spare a valium
For your unmarried sister?
I get the frighteners when I scream
At my baby in her baby rocker.

Or a sweet-box of affection;
Or a coal-bag of laughter;
Or a bottle of sodium amytol —
I am worn out by it all.

I'm a friend with no friend —
But don't get me wrong:
I prefer life to death
But the pain is too strong.

I adore the trees in the park
But I'm no nature lover:
It's a boy in the factory —
He won't let me get closer.

I don't want him to marry me;
I don't want him to live with me;
I want him only to sleep with me,
Sleep with me, and drown me.

The factory smoke is halcyon
In the blue city air;
Brother, can you spare a valium
For a lonely bear?

The gossips are a-huntin'
With a high moral gun;
A trapped she-bear in Cabra
Is their idea of fun.

Brother, can you spare a valium?
I'm too low to get high;
I don't want to go to heaven,
I don't want to die.

I'm a friend with no friend –
But don't get me wrong:
I prefer life to death
But the pain is too strong.

A WEDDING IN RANELAGH, SUMMER, 1982

Into the canal-lock at Charlemont Bridge
Boys and girls dive in their jeans:
— Carmel, will you put your ear to the water and listen?
— Shay, will you teach me how to do the backstroke?
When the last lock-keeper died
They decided that he — he was buried in Mount Jerome —
Would be the last lock-keeper.
Who are 'They'? The more I see of 'Them'
— Usually under the toenails of the Central Bank —
I get the wind up me.
The last lock-keeper was seven foot tall —
A tall man who lived alone with a sheepdog
Because the woman he had loved had written to him
She loved him so much she could not live with him
And she had emigrated to Skopje in Yugoslavia.
He was a character — as they say — not because he was mad
But because he was sane;
Because he was the heart and soul of Charlemont Bridge
And his humour was a byword as was his courtesy;
Who loved nothing more than on August afternoons to watch
Boys and girls mating in the lock;
The white bodies down in the black clay of the steep waters
And, in the tossing sunlight, their bunched cauliflower heads.
He used say:
"If there be a God — and funny enough I believe that there be —
He is a young mother in Moore Street arguing the toss
Over the price and the weight of two heads of cauliflower:
That's who God is — a young mother in Moore Street — Imagine!"

In a cold water, high ceilinged, one-room flat
Overlooking Charlemont Bridge,
A young priest meets again and again his Skopje girl;
Marries again and again his parnel bride;
On his back in the court of her power,
In the spume of her source;
The font:
The shoemaker's wife died in her sleep last night
And early this morning her seventh grand-daughter was born.
The lock swimmers dive yet again:
And her legs around his waist,

Each a steeplejack of their own fountain;
Making spray, like hay, in the evening city sunlight:
They climb to their feet and put on their shoes
And walk down Ranelagh to have a drink in Humphrey's:
There is a red helicopter over Portobello
And the boys and the girls are already sitting up at the counter:
A wedding breakfast about to begin!

THE FAREWELL TO BALLYMUN BY GOYA

10.15 a.m. — it is time to go:
I loom in the door, not wanting to go:
Of my dilemma, God ought to know —

Yet nobody is taking the barest notice:
Not the barest, Maria, not the barest:
Not one Special Branch man here to hold my hand.

10.15 a.m. and you are asleep in your bed
By the wide window: 4.30 a.m. —
When you came in from your nightshift —

You made coffee for the pair of us
And curled up beside me. Asleep in one another,
We swam in the coves of Donegal:

Sitting up in the sand, glancing each other in the eyes:
Your sheep's eyes, all rocks and water:
I had a nightmare about a Round Tower in Kildare.

I loom in the door, wanting only to wake you:
To wake you from your secret, copper-mine sleep:
To ask yet again for your affection and solace.

For the last time I glance back at you:
At your sleeping face in the bombed-out city:
Seven storeys up in the t-shaped tower.

Your sleeping face is the sun in the cloud:
In the pillow of cloud the buried sun of your face!
Your face — the sun — which comes and which goes.

The Knife of the Snow Dance — with serrated edges:
You surge across the dance floor to meet me on the rocks:
You surge back across the dance floor to strand me on the rocks.

You who for twenty-seven years I searched:
Across the railway tracks of your sleeping face
A red-haired railwayman in blue overalls

Shakes hands with me precariously:
Sad, orange moustache; curly hair uncombed:
A satchel of tools strapped on to his back.

By the dirty, silver ear-ring at the side of your face
A driver in his loco is checking his lunchbox:
A young mother in Beirut in the Cedars of Lebannon

Plucks her baby from the corpse of her spouse:
In war and peace you are always you:
Which opens up my heart as I stare back at you asleep.

I shut your door, cross the platform, climb into the train:
A child in the dark asks: Will somebody switch on the light?
A businessman has fears of being tied up in a deal coffin.

A meek nun explodes: "He is the kind of man, Sister Pat,
Who tries to tell you Everything in five minutes flat."
Sleep, O my *compañero*, sleep! Sleep the sleep of the dead!

Waken to the sun at noon being emptied over your head
By Dublin coalmen, binmen, postmen:
Behold thyself in thy window and spill over with smiles:

Jump from the window — but inwards not outwards:
Think of your Goya — what a secretive guy:
A blood-woman like you should live ten thousand years!

DAVE LOVES MACKER 14.2.83.

When you fall in love, you fall:
Fall into water — deep water.
You know that you are out of your depth
But that that does not matter
Because you know also that you are both drowning.

When you fall in love, you fall:
Fall into the dream of a long life livid with love.
The dream, which is itself a drowning on a dangerous shore,
Is that you will keep on drowning to the end of time;
That this drowning together will never end.

When Dave fell for Macker, Dave fell:
Fell into a nosedive into her lips and eyes;
The further they kissed the further away swam her face;
Her thighs, like her mind, all in a tangle of seaweed;
Beautiful seaweed, all slippery-gold, hairy-green.

When they fell, they fell into pow-wow:
Fell into silence — the music of sex.
They embraced upside-down and she pursed her mouth
Like a wide-eyed trout with its tail up in the air
Who does not believe in the existence of fishermen.

When they fell, they fell into silence:
Fell into a for-real pow-wow: a strange language.
When Dave said "Do you love me, Macker?"
She laughed and she laughed and she laughed
"None of that now — you're a good bloke to drown with."

As Dave fell downwards, Macker fell upwards:
Fell upwards into the light of another man's eyes
While Dave fell downwards into the darkness of hers.
Now only their entwined ankles held them together:
Lobsters in lobsterpots laughed — "We are amused."

When Macker fell upwards, Macker fell upwards:
Fell like she felt she was the Queen of Mozambique
Or Donnybrook — in sombrero and thighboots.
When Dave fell downwards, Dave fell downwards:
Fell like he felt he was airborne in stone.

When you drown in love, you drown:
Drown in a drowning from which there is no rescue;
To which both of you demand to be doomed;
Your bodies not to be exhumed for a hundred years;
Found neck in neck at the bottom of the sea.

When you fall out of love, you fall out:
Fall out into an ocean-wave which eats you up
Or into rocks which slash you with razors.
Better if nobody finds you — your loneliness is leprous;
You have swallowed too much — too much salt water.

When you fall out of love, you fall out:
Fall out into the asphalt of a disused pool
By whose edge in the sunny breeze together you exulted
When it was full and the pair of you mistook
A corporation swimming-pool for the Indian Ocean.

When you fall in love, you fall:
Two drowned corpses prowling in a snowed-under graveyard
Where the sunken headstones are slumped spectators in thick,
                                        white coats.
You stalk each other with all the emnity of pain:
When you fall in love, you fall.

THE ATHLONE YEARS

Neither of us had been in Athlone before —
Mother and I: we decided to stay two nights
In *The Sunshine Hotel* — excellently appointed
For her to binocularise the cloud-eaten skies
And to camera-snap the raindrops on the windowpane.
At the end of the first day we concurred
That Mullingar was 'not a patch' on Athlone —
As Mother put it. On the second day
We met for luncheon in *Les Enfants du Paradis,*
A barn-size restaurant on Church Street
Owned by the Lukers, a distinguished farming family.
"Will you please stop staring at our waitress"
Mother whispered to me under the crimson menu-card;
"Or, if you cannot help it, at least do so discreetly."
That afternoon, as we explored Athlone Castle —
With its spectacular museum of agricultural implements —
I could see only the signature of the waitress at the foot of the bill:
"Table No 7: Caroline Tormey":
When a human being who is a woman smiles from the heart,
Not from the streetcorners of her mouth or from the drawbridges
                                                    of her eyes,
Then it seems to me that I have scaled the Seven-Storey Mountain
And I get a cheekbone-glimpse of the paradise
— A place unlike the world, much like the earth.
Mother barked: "Over here is a mantrap — the genuine article"
And, as I peered at the teeth of the mantrap, the image enlarged
Of a tall human being in a black skirt and white blouse;
Small, gold ear-rings in her ears, a bunch of keys at her waist;
Hips branching out from her, and shoulders with leaves;
A tree stalking the skyline past immobile deer;
She was a faun who had become a pine.
"You're getting on my nerves, boy" Mother sniffed
"See you back at *The Sunshine* for dinner at eight."
Across the alley at the back-door of *Les Enfants du Paradis*
The river horripilated — yes — in the sun;
A yellow brute of a man — one of the proprietors —
Mistook me for a priest and said "Certainly, Father"
When I asked "May I speak to Caroline Tormey?"
I said "What time do you finish?" — "4.30" she said;
I said "I'll be waiting at the quay wall."

She smiled unexpectedly and blew back into the dark.
At 4.32 I felt a hand on my shoulder
And I saw two smiles on her face like two rainbows in the same sky:
"Do you know somewhere quiet where we could have a drink?"
I began — but at 6 p.m. when the angelus tolled
We were still standing at the quay wall, discussing
The difference between bollards and capstans.
I returned to Athlone two weeks later
And — in spite of the architecture and in spite of the taboos —
We lived together in Athlone for seven years
Until now Caroline has decided that she wants to go to Spain;
And — she believes — our children will bloom in Spain.
Now, as I write, I am crouched
On a bench across the river from *Les Enfants du Paradis:*
Across the stern of a dredger
I catch a glimpse of Caroline Tormey on the far side of the river;
My instinct is to cry to her but I know I must not;
Oh! River of Solitude between a Man and a Woman;
Dear heart, only life — not death — can do us part:
It is — and yet it is not — a time to be smart
When a human being who is a woman smiles from the heart.

BLIND YOUNG MAN, VIRGINIA

Where I pitch my perch in the middle of O'Connell Street Bridge
I like always to place a transistor radio behind my head:
My begging bowl is a biscuit tin
And I rattle it to the rhythm of the music on the airwaves:
I sport dark shades but I do not pack a white stick:
Some people, of course, opine that I am a con
But I have been blind since birth, never seen nothing
Except a mess of light — a visual soup
That means no more to me that it would to you.
When the noise of the traffic gets bad I switch up the volume:
I could not do my begging except to the sound of music.
Back at home
When the Mamas and the Papas
(That's what we call them)
Want to punish me
They confiscate my transistor radio.
I believe that if I listen to music for long enough
Suddenly the woman
— Is it necessary for me to say it, for Christ's sake, is it? —
Of whom I dream night and day
Will land into the solar plexus of O'Connell Street Bridge
And say something like — "You look wrecked" —
To which I will reply — "Do I? That's great" —
And in among the shynesses
(You got shyness trouble too? Good)
One of us will invite the other to have a cup of coffee
In some nice dive in O'Connell Street.

That is exactly what happend on the first day in June:
She's a fiddler
In the North Dublin City Symphony Orchestra
— First violin —
And when she brings me out to meet her mother in Howth,
Where they live together in a bungalow overlooking Ireland's Eye,
Her mother naturally is pretty afraid for her daughter
And she is not re-assured by all the black coffee I drink
And my talk of cliffs — how I love to go for cliffwalks —
(Truth is that I have never been on a cliff in my life —
Only read about cliff-roads on the coasts of Yugoslavia):
If I was Virginia's mother I too would be pretty afraid:

Blind young man, with not a penny to my name —
And if we have children, will the children be blind?
Oh God! Are you really God? Or are you, like Santa Claus,
A creation of the Black Forest — an Imaginary Bear?
If I was Virginia's mother I'd be pretty scared — wouldn't you?
Nearly every day now for the last three months
Me and Virginia have met and sometimes she says to me:
"When you're ready, Jack, come in off the bridge":
And I say to her
"I've got my eye on Ireland's Eye":
And she says to me, convoluted with chuckles,
"Say that again, Jack, say that again";
And I do, and I do, and I do —
I take off my shades and I close my eyes
And I say it for Virginia, I say it again:
I've got my eye on Ireland's Eye —
I've got my eye on Ireland's Eye.

THE BABY GIRAFFE

Just as we were about to say goodbye for the last time
— Extricating ourselves from the car-crash of a tragic friendship —
I happened to mention — I don't know why —
Perhaps it was the lettuce-patch I had seen in her garden —
That when I was a boy I had a baby giraffe.
The way she circled my face with her eyes —
You'd think I'd said I'd had thirty-seven legs.
What age were you? — she asked. Fourteen — I replied.
What colour was it? — she asked. Orange — I replied.
Will you stay for tea? — she asked. I will — I replied.
And as she cut the brown bread and poured out the tea
She inquired if I had a place to stay for the night.
As she fucked me under a full moon, she laughed —
'You are not the only fourteen-year old with a baby giraffe.'

TRINITY COLLEGE DUBLIN, 1983

I don't think you know what cobblestones are . . .
I think that it is just that you like the sound of the words:
Look, do you see that girl over there in the blue jacket?
The tall girl . . . yes . . . in the red slippers?
With the small bloke in the long black overcoat?
Do you know that in her life — she's about twenty-seven —
She has made love about nine hundred times
Whereas he to whom she is talking
— He's about forty-three —
He has made love about five — maybe ten — times?
The reason that he is lying flat on his back on the ground
And that she is standing with one foot on his forehead
Is that he's crazy about her and she's not altogether quite sane about him:
That's what cobblestones are for; that's what cobblestones are.

THE PEDESTRIANISATION OF GRAFTON STREET

I liked him something fierce — although he was an awful eejit.
I mean: he could never keep his mouth shut
So that while he was an entertaining conversationalist
He was always putting his foot in it, dropping clangers,
And even out walking he'd keep on talking
And frequently fall off the footpath or bump into a lamp-post:
The big snag was that he wanted me to go to bed with him
And, worst of all, I think he really was — in love with me.
The last straw was the Pedestrianisation of Grafton Street:
Now we were to spend our days walking up and down Grafton Street
And our nights in a big brass bed in the middle of Grafton Street:
When I wake up in the mornings I realise I'm not dreaming:
I'm in Grafton Street and he's talking — about the Pedestrianisation
                                                                of Rome.

THE SLEEPING ARRANGEMENTS

Then it came time to go to bed and she led me into a room
With a double-bed and I was smiling — my sole anxiety being
Which side of the bed I should sleep in.
'Surely you can decide at least that much for yourself':
She laughed that big, country, collective laugh of hers.
Casually I remarked — as if it did not matter to me —
'And where are you sleeping yourself?'
'In the room at the far end of the passage from you' —
And she looked into my eyes and she kissed me on the cheek.
Alone in the bedroom, I stood on my head in the corner;
Until I felt it was safe to slip out of the house.
Then, I ran screaming through the streets to the railway station:
Nobody took any notice of me, except the silent streets.

THE LION TAMER

'Well, what do you work at?' she said to me after about six months
Of what a mutual journalist friend was pleased to call our 'relationship';
'I'm a lion tamer' I replied, as off-handedly as possible,
Hoping she'd say 'Are you really?'
Instead she said: 'I don't believe you'.
So I jumped up from my chair and I strode across the room
(Knocking over a wicker-work magazine-rack by accident)
And I knelt on one knee at her feet and gazed up at her:
Slowly she edged away from me and backed out the door
And glancing out the window I saw her bounding down the road,
Her fair hair gleaming in the wind, her crimson voice growling.
I kicked over a stool and threw my whip on the floor.
What I had hoped for from her was a thorough mauling.
But she preferred artistic types. She had no appetite for lion tamers.

THE LAST HALLO

When she showed me into the living-room of her suburban villa
I jumped up on a bookshelf, hoping she'd join me;
Instead she sat in a bean-bag and chain-smoked,
Talking about books and shelves and all that kind of thing.
Then when upstairs on the bus into town I sat at the back
She sat up-front and when the ticket-collector came
I said to him, pointing up the whole long length of the bus,
"*I'm* with *her*";
We got off the bus at different stops in Harcourt Street
And we walked through the Green on opposite sides of the path;
In The Unicorn Restaurant she cancelled her booking for a table for two
And in College Green we waited at the same stop for different buses:
Hers came first and meaning to say Goodbye she smiled and said Hallo.
Hallo — I replied, as she climbed into the sky. Goodbye Hallo.

PHONE 506440 OR ANY GARDA STATION

Nobody knows where's Emily —
Even the Guards are getting scared:
Nobody knows where's Emily —
As if anybody ever cared!

Only Emily knows who Emily is —
She is a law unto herself:
No one cares about anyone else
Except in relation to oneself.

Emily's father and mother used run
A concentration camp for lucky children:
Emily, honour they father and mother!
Why should I? I do not like them.

Emily's husband is a teacher
Who develops property on the moon:
"It is only I who can reach her —
Only I who can prick her balloon."

He chalks her name on the blackboard — EM —
"When chalk snaps, is that an omen?
Or some kind of esoteric equation?"
He scratches his groin in anticipation.

Emily sees what they don't see —
That Loneliness is The Big Machine:
J.C.B. in a real field —
Solution to a Cowslip's dream.

EM and ILY equals Emily —
Or does it? Her head adorns
The motorway, while among the thorns
Her torso without moving swims.

Coming down the road to kiss Emily —
On her breasts and on her lips:
Coming down the road to eat Emily —
Her big breasts and her big lips.

I will make certain to gobble her wings —
Spitting out the pips:
I will make certain to gobble her wings —
Spitting out the pips.

Gravy, gravy, gravy, gravy,
A little girl with a balloon:
Blood, blood, blood, blood,
A little girl with a balloon.

Nobody knows where's Emily —
Even the Guards are getting scared:
Nobody knows where's Emily —
As it anybody ever cared!

THE GOLDEN GIRL

Yes I knew her once — The Golden Girl —
Strange name — she dressed always in black —
Leading a camel through St Stephen's Green —
Teaching ballet to a farmer in Parnell Square —
Hunting for bus-stops at night in O'Connell Street —
Like the gold lunula hanging on the blackthorn tree,
Which was which? Was it the black tree
That, in the dying sun, was the most golden of all?
She was the black tree — The Golden Girl:
And she was called by that name
Because she was what she was —
She walked always in circles in a straight line.

The Golden Girl — and you could say —
Yes you could say — she had a heart of gold:
Which was why there was always a Gold Rush
Of Blokes, crazily panning the streets for her:
Yet when one of them — I speak of myself —
Came face to face with her
— Gazing down the gravel of her eyes —
Her heart of gold slipped through my fingers
And her deadpan humour left me standing still:
She was called by that name
Because she was what she was —
She walked always in circles in a straight line.

If you should see her photograph in a magazine
Cut it out — and pencil in the date —
And place it tenderly in your most cherished book
— *Tarry Flynn* by Patrick Kavanagh —
But remember that, in spite of her laughing eyes
And her mouth with its puzzled frown,
It bears no resemblance to the actual girl —
To the real Golden Girl
Whom on this earth you will never know:
She was called by that name
Because she was what she was —
She walked always in circles in a straight line.

One day Michelangelo — or was it Picasso? —
I forget which — it does not matter —
One of the big boys — all his admirers
Round him in the art gallery on whose dirty floor
The Golden Girl knelt with a portfolio of her drawings:
What was evident was not that she was beautiful
Which she was but that her drawings — unnoticed —
Were more subtle, more muscular,
Than the works of the big boys, and her eyes were tears.
She was called by that name
— Because she was what she was —
She walked always in circles in a straight line.

Now — it is time to paint the gate:
The gate that will not lock:
Now it is time to speak of love —
Love swinging in the wind:
The State has disappeared but she has remained,
And there are no newspapers — only her eyes;
And behind her the sea — the waiting sea:
The sea waiting to enter the city
Like sleep into the head of a child:
And she was called by that name
Because she was what she was —
She walked always in circles in a straight line.

GOING HOME TO MEET SYLVIA

I

I am going down the road with Sylvia;
And I will not be going home;
I am going down the road with Sylvia;
And I will not be going home.

II

I will be going to the Carnival with Sylvia;
I hope to meet nobody there;
I will be going to the Carnival with Sylvia;
I hope to meet nobody there.

III

I am going down the road to meet Sylvia;
Sylvia is not going to meet me;
I will be coming back down the road from Sylvia;
And I will not be going home.

IV

I am going down the road with Sylvia;
And I will not be going home;
I am going down the road with Sylvia;
And I will not be going home.